Praise for ꞏꞏꞏ꞉ d

"I know I will keep ꞏꞏꞏ ꞏg
time to come, if not ꞏꞏꞏ
sheer GENIUS!"   — ꞏꞏꞏjters, The Netherlands

"I have been doing dialogues with myself and have had some quite startling realizations. It is clearly a very powerful tool!"
                                            — Randy Austill

"Reading Bruce's book was one of the most profound experiences of my life. I got through 30 pages the first night, had intense and 'insightful' dreams and awoke to a transformed world."   — Sue Kranz, Canada

"The Option idea is a very powerful one and it has had a strong impact on my life."   — John McIlroy

"Bruce's words are inspiring and I will keep them close to remind me of the source of my happiness and my choice to claim my right to perfect peace and joy!"
                                        — Geraldine Berbaum

"I was so amazed to learn about this method and how easy it can be to become happy."
                                    — Lutz Stradmann, Germany

"Bruce and Deborah have given the world a GREAT gift."
                                        — Bob Marino

"Bruce, our dear, dear friend . . . Through the years, your 'gifts' have been plentiful, yet incalculable — since through them, we have had the opportunity to re-weave the very fabric of our lives — in every way. There will never be a way we could demonstrate or give enough to fully express the extent of our appreciation and gratitude for your existence . . . but we do experience it for ourselves every day of our lives! All Light & Love."   — Bears & Samahria

Also by Bruce Di Marsico and Deborah Mendel

Unlock Your Happiness
With Five Simple Questions

The
Option
Method

Bruce M. Di Marsico

Embrace your specialness. You have
within you the seeds for a beautiful
garden. Spread them fearlessly.

Dragonfly Press

Published by Dragonfly Press
C/O Deborah Mendel
P.O. Box 1192
Walnut Grove, CA 95690

Illustrations and Cover Art: Chris Spencer
Edited by: Deborah Mendel

ISBN: 0-9704795-5-7

Library of Congress Control Number: 2004100709

Second Edition
Originally entitled *The Principles and Philosophy of The Option Method*

Printed and bound in the United States of America by
Morris Publishing • *www.morrispublishing.com* • 800-650-7888

1 2 3 4 5 6 7 8 9 10

I would like to dedicate this book to all of the Option students everywhere around the world. To all of our "Monday Night" gang, those dear ones who have passed on, and those who remain, I hope this book is a wish finally fulfilled. For those of you who never had the opportunity to know Bruce personally, may it bring you that much closer to a man I'm sure you would have loved. Let it empower you and inspire you to share the joy in your hearts.

TANTRA -

Is it sacred?

Is it sacred sexuality?

Are you gifting out of
pure love - healing with
~~escstasy~~ Ecstacy - Extatic Energy?

Are you receiving as a pure
gift of love?

This is not about sex, or
romance. It is about
Sharing energy, in a pure
state - healing, expanding,
growing in light & love.

It is a powerful energy,
and misused - or used with
the wrong intensions it
can, and will cause harm.
You have to approach in
- pure giving or receiving state.

To approach Tantra as sex, or even better sex, is to miss the point.

This is not about new partners, getting a little extra, or on the side. It is not to be trifled with.

Used out of integrity, is a form of rape - robot sex.

When you come from an open heart, a gifting heart - gifting your heart to the other - purely - The joy and healing can be extreme, immense.

This is not about Technique. Technique is only open the energy channels, so the pure, raw, healing energies can flow.

Look inside your heart. If it is about you. Stop. Reconsider your intentions. If you cannot

come from pure, gifting love.
STOP.
To go forward will ~~diminish~~
diminish you and your partner.
It will Take, Not Heal.

Whether giver or receiver.
STOP.
Put yourself in a pure state.

If you can not. Tell you
partner. Take care of
Them. Gift Them with
love, with holding, but
not with Tantra Love
making. Let This act of
honesty and authenticity
be your gift of love.

Your intentions & heart
must be pure to proceed.

Contents

"Quid Querits . . . What do you seek?"
This is the age-old question posed to those who seek a new way of life. It is a question for those who are seeking more satisfaction by finding better ways of expressing and enjoying their deeply held truths and insights. Through the Option Method I have found new happiness, and the knowledge that real and lasting happiness is possible.

— **Bruce Di Marsico**

Foreword

Thirty-seven years ago a young man was establishing a private counseling practice on the east coast. Through his experiences with clients and his own self-exploration, he was beginning to formulate his own insights into the reasons why people were unhappy. One day a teaching position fell into his lap. The year was 1970. The human potential movement was under way. Most of the movement's concepts we take for granted today, in this age of self-awareness and self-improvement, but at the time this movement was new and exciting.

The young man was Bruce M. Di Marsico. He was requested to present a program outline to teach a class at a new school that was just opening in New York City. The school was called G.R.O.W. or Group Relations Ongoing Workshops. G.R.O.W. offered certificates and training exclusively in such subjects as Group Encounter, Psychodrama, Gestalt Therapy, Sensitivity Training, Existential Analysis, and much more.

Bruce realized he had something new and unique to offer in this field and he jumped at the opportunity, quickly formulating a name and outline for his course. He had until then never called his technique anything, but now it became necessary to name it. The foundation of his approach to helping people was based on his recognition that people were unhappy because they believed that they should be. He understood that people believed that it was good and necessary to feel bad. Bruce believed that people had a choice when it came to their emotions. As he reflected on this concept, it came to him: choice = option = Option Method. Option Method was born and he submitted his course proposal. Option Method was added to G.R.O.W.'s curriculum. Bruce introduced the Option Method to the public.

Bruce didn't know it yet but he was about to become one of the most popular teachers at G.R.O.W. Soon there was standing room only in his classrooms. Word was out about this exciting new method and self-help tool and the unique man teaching it.

Bruce's students asked for more classes and he began a series of programs in his house in Montclair, New Jersey. He wrote almost daily about happiness and unhappiness. Writing was his form of meditation and contemplation. He naturally wrote for his students in preparation for workshops and groups. Themes evolved weekly in lectures and essays. His students returned again and again, eager to hear their teacher talk about what he had written. He wanted so much to teach them what he himself was learning in this process. In each lesson he tried to crystallize and further clarify the basic principles of his Option Method.

Bruce was a philosopher, theologian, and storyteller. He loved to philosophize, analyze, and conceptualize. He could entertain an atheist with his interpretation of Biblical tales, Jesus Christ and God, but it was his own personal quest for spiritual and emotional peace that moved him to write.

I first met Bruce in the basement of the house that would become my home. We were introduced by a mutual friend. Bruce had a small studio in his basement where he played with any number of artistic endeavors. He dabbled in woodcarving, jewelry making, sculpting and painting, to name a few. I did not know much about him at the time other than he helped people to become happier.

Our mutual friend called out to him as we descended the basement stairs that day. As I watched Bruce emerge from a narrow passageway out his studio I found myself overwhelmed by his captivating smile and his warm and loving spirit. It was love at first sight. I had never felt more loved and accepted in those brief moments of our first meeting than in my entire life. I was drawn to him instantly.

I would come to spend the next twenty-two years of my life with him. I had the immeasurable joy of watching him teach, heal and inspire so many people. Bruce and his Option Method became my life. I hope to share with you in this book a glimpse of Bruce, his fundamental teachings, his visions and understanding of unhappiness and happiness, and his Option Method.

I have taken two booklets, which Bruce wrote for the last workshop he taught before his death, and combined them in this one volume. They were originally titled "The Basis" and "A Brief Compendium of the Option Method." I asked my friend, artist, and Option Method student Jennifer Hautman to help me to rearrange and commingle Bruce's material. My dear friend, poet and educator Frank Niccoletti worked by my side, helping me to edit Bruce's writing. I have also added in italics, before each chapter, some of my favorite quotes of Bruce's taken from various other lectures.

Be patient with yourself and Bruce as you read these chapters. Bruce loved to exhaust "all the angles" and to explore. You may find that you need to re-read some portions or paragraphs while others may immediately strike a chord that vibrates deep in your heart.

My intention here is to create a study book for Option Method students who may want to share it with others. I also envision this book as an invaluable tool in workshops or groups for learning the basic principles and philosophy of the Option Method as Bruce Di Marsico himself originally taught it. However you use this book, I know Bruce would have wanted you to enjoy it.

— Deborah Mendel

Acknowledgments

I would like to thank Frank Niccoletti for never letting me quit, no matter how much I tried to do so. His dedication to this book and to keeping Bruce's voice alive, though he had never met Bruce, was inspiring.

I would like to thank Jennifer Hautman for all of her creative efforts and enthusiasm. Many thanks to Mandy Evans for her encouragement, advice, wisdom and kindness.

A special thanks and recognition to my dear friend John Salacan, who introduced me to Bruce so long ago. John was Bruce's right hand man, sounding board, fellow explorer and business partner. He was witness to Bruce's unfolding revelations and discoveries as he developed the Option Method in the early 1970's. John had an enduring love and dedication to Bruce and what became his life's work. I hope this book pleases him, that it will warm his heart to finally see at least some of Bruce's work published.

My love always to Wendy Dolber for her endless patience and eternal friendship. Bruce always loved her sharp wit and admired her writing talents. She brings both these and her own special gifts to her work with Option. I'd like to express my profound gratitude to Russell Ooms for always listening, for being my personal cheering section, the one who helped me across the gulf between death and my life.

Message From The Designer

I was introduced to Option in March of 1995. Up until then I had been searching my whole life for a way to raise my self-esteem, overcome my fears and achieve my dreams. Bottom line: what I really wanted was to be happy. Option helped me to achieve this like none of the hundreds of self-help books, tapes and personal growth seminars I had consumed for nearly 15 years. It has changed my experience of life so profoundly that I refer to time as "before and after Option."

Although the Option Method has been compared to many different types of psychotherapies, it is radically different than anything I had ever experienced. It's the only process I've found that not only helped me to change my mind, but to create visible differences in my life. I have been amazed by its simplicity and innocence, but most significantly by its effectiveness.

Unfortunately, I never had the opportunity to meet Bruce Di Marsico but I was excited to find his wife and partner Debbie. We formed a friendship and co-created a web site called *optionmethodnetwork.com*, which promotes Option and its practitioners. I was thrilled when she asked me to work with her on this book. Ever since my exposure to this method, I've been a staunch advocate for the Option Method. This opportunity has beautifully combined my years of experience as a graphic artist with my passion for the Option Method and its principles.

The challenge in organizing Bruce's work to form this book had to do with his style of communicating. Bruce was an intelligent man and philosopher who wrote in what I call "philosophical speak." It takes a certain degree of focused concentration to understand the profound wisdom behind his words.

I hope you enjoy the material and find it useful. Changing the beliefs that are causing you pain is where the rubber really hits the road. I hope you use this material to instigate having your own Option Method dialogue because real change doesn't happen until it's personal.

Enjoy.

— Jennifer Hautman

Unlock Your Happiness
With Five Simple Questions

The
Option
Method

A Message From Bruce

Because the basic idea of Option is simple, the insights of the Option Method can be expressed in many cases as aphorisms. The goal in this exposition is to be succinct. In most sections the ideas expressed are merely restatements of another idea, or the same central truth. I realize that there is really only one truth of happiness and that truth can be expressed in various ways. My hope is to try to be relevant to the concerns of the different kinds of reader, whether he/she is a curious person, a novice, an advanced student or an Option Practitioner.

I intend this manual to be easy to use for a more effective practice of the Option Method. In no way is it meant to or is it able to supplant the personal experience of using the Option Method. It is a practical handbook for the application of what you may already know. When a reminder is not pertinent or useful, nothing can substitute for the Option Method itself.

Those who hope to help others can especially benefit from the knowledge that there is, indeed, a canon of truisms about happiness, unhappiness, and the many names unhappiness goes by. If what, at first, seems too dogmatic and simplistic in my style puts you off, please be patient. I only mean to make a cogent whole out of many years of experience, and various attempts to teach the Option Method in the most effective way. This material is meant as a teaching guide. Although I hope it can be used to answer most questions, I know that there are areas I have not even touched on, let alone exhausted.

In any case, when the various sections are studied and explored, in no particular order if you wish, I think that an understanding of the Option Method's simplicity will emerge. The ideal aim of using this guide is to further your own explorations and expertise in the employment of the Option Method. This is the best use it could have. Your life as a happy person is the only life you truly want. This material is dedicated to the fact that happiness is really your option. I hope Option will be your way to know that.

Have fun with the ideas in here.

— Bruce Di Marsico

Embrace your specialness. You have within you the seeds for a beautiful garden. Spread them fearlessly. Your seeds are not able to grow into ugly plants, but only seeds of fruits. Some seeds will only seem not to grow, others will seem to need extra care, and others will disappear and grow where you may never see the fruit. But wherever they take root, and for however short a time they may seem to grow, know that from them came something that there never was before.

1

All People Seek Happiness

What is the purpose or meaning of life? Each person will answer this for himself or herself. How you answer determines how you live. This life means your life. It does not have to be other than what it is. But since all want true happiness, by whatever name, one could suppose that unless the decided purpose of your life is happiness, it would not seem to be a happy life unless you had what you wanted.

What is the purpose or meaning of your life? Is the purpose of your life to be happy, or would you prefer your life to be for something else, or nothing? Would that make you happy? Whatsoever you seek, you still seek the cessation of unhappiness and the satisfaction of happiness.

What do you believe is preventing you from being happy? Do you need to see more justice in the world? After you have justice, what would you feel? Happy? After truth? After health? After riches? After charity? After peace on earth? Then will your happiness be allowed?

Happiness for the good and punishment for the evil? After you have your wishes, what would you be? Happy? Any goal or ideal is the means through which you are ultimately seeking happiness. You believe these things are necessary first. If you don't believe true happiness is possible or desirable without them, why?

Using an extreme example: Are there people who would be willing to die, even to save another? If there are, then that idea of seeing themselves as loving the other so much, even to self-sacrifice, makes them happy. You do all that you do for happiness. You may not have realized that.

Your Right to Happiness

We all have the right to be happy. All people are allowed to be happy at all times, forever. This is happiness—to know you are always allowed to be happy no matter who you are, what you do and no matter what happens to you. All people have the right to be happy. It is never wrong to be happy. Those who know it are happy forever.

You have the right to be happy no matter how rotten others think you are—no matter how sinful, or stupid, or selfish, or sick, or horrible, or thieving, or lying, or arrogant, or shy, or failing, or murderous, or monstrous. You absolutely have the absolute right to be happy always—no matter how others may hate you, or hurt you, or try to punish you. Those who disagree will be unhappy.

Blessed are those who know they are happy. Happy are those who know they are blessed. To be blessed is to have the right to be happy. To be born is to be allowed to be happy. To know you are allowed to be happy is to be blessed.

Happiness is being allowed to be happy. Happiness is acknowledging it can never be wrong to be happy. Happiness is knowing you will be happy in the future. Happiness is realizing that there could never be a time when you should be unhappy. Happiness is what is left when you stop believing you have to be unhappy. Happiness is knowing it is okay to be happy.

God permits you to be happy *no matter what or when*. Nature permits you to be happy *no matter what or when*. The only permission you need is yours to be happy all the time. You don't have to deny your happiness ever. It is not wrong to be happy always.

You Can Be Happy

Happiness is being glad for who you are. It is admitting that . . .

* You like that you want what you want.
* You like that you don't like what you don't like.
* You like that you change your mind whenever you think that is best.
* You like that you don't change your mind until you really change your mind.
* You like that you don't like not knowing how to have what you want.
* You like that you don't like being mistaken.
* You like that you feel just the way you like to feel about everything you do.
* You like that you feel just the way you like to feel about everything that happens.

However you have been, considering what you believed, and how you perceived things . . . You couldn't have been different. If that helps you understand your life, it is because it is true. If that feels relieving, or like forgiveness, that is because it is true.

True forgiveness is knowing that there is nothing to forgive.

2

The Option Method Questions

In this method we use the word unhappiness merely as a model word to discuss all kinds of feelings that people describe variously as bad emotional feelings. We mean to include any emotions or feelings ranging from mild annoyance to murderous rage—from disappointment to suicidal depression. When dealing with a specific person's feelings, we use the descriptive word or terminology of the person who is unhappy.

* What are you unhappy about?
* What [is it] about that, that makes you unhappy?
* Why are you unhappy about that?
* What are you afraid would happen if you were not unhappy about that? *or*
* What are you afraid it would mean if you were not unhappy about that?
* Why do you believe it would mean that?

(A detailed model of the application of the Option Method questions is provided in Chapter 8. Readers may turn to it at any time.)

The whole subject of happiness and unhappiness is what the Option Method is about. Each person and all mankind can always be happy and never be unhappy again. Since we choose our emotions, we have the option to be happy. How can you decide to be happy? You can expect to be happier and want to be. Since absolutely nothing has the power to prevent it, you will be. Know that you can always be happy because absolutely nothing can make you unhappy.

This is the Option invitation:
If you want to be happy, be happy.
If you don't believe you can be happy,
use the Option Method to feel better.

Although there is much to learn about the Option Method and its many applicable concepts, there is nothing didactic[1] about the Option Method as a method. It is first, and foremost, and solely an analytic technique, a maieutic[2] and heuristic[3] method of questioning. Its heuristic quality is what makes it the Option Method. I never intended to create it as a preaching procedure or a way to tell people that they need not be unhappy. The Option

1   didactic — intended to teach
2   maieutic — method of questioning by which Socrates brought a person to consciousness of latent knowledge
3   heuristic — useful for discovering knowledge

Method is a helpful tool meant to aid people in discovering for themselves what their role is in their happiness and unhappiness.

The individual is the sole determiner of his or her emotional state. This underlying rationale must be accepted as indisputable by those who wish to practice the Option Method with others. The proper application of the Option Method requires this knowledge. The Option Method Practitioner, when using the Option Method, never teaches, advises, or challenges the client. Self-analysis and discovery are the value of the Option Method.

I created the Option Method to reveal what beliefs are operative in an unhappy person. This simple questioning method disclosed to the sufferers that they are the determiner of their feelings. It shows that they are feeling exactly what they believe they should feel, always.

It just so happens that when people realize they have a choice in their emotions, it makes a difference to them. People are only unhappy when they believe it is necessary. The question, of course, is when is it necessary? It is this question that the Option Method explores.

By using the Option Method we will be able to see these dynamics at work in ourselves. We will allow ourselves to discover in actual practice, by personal experience, the role we play in our own emotions, and then be able to see more clearly who we really are and how we really feel. Happy.

About Beliefs

A belief is assuming something to be true, to be fact. A belief is not caused, it is created by choice. A belief *about* a thing's existence is not the same as its existence. A belief is what a person assumes or holds to be true. What is, is. What is not, is not. Beliefs about what is, or is not, are merely beliefs. They only have a kind of experiential, functional existence. A self-affirmed belief is not the proof of truth. Illusions of truth or reality are not the experience of truth or reality, but the experience of the beliefs about truth and reality.

Merely *believing* that something can cause unhappiness makes you feel it can and will cause unhappiness. Merely *believing* something is making you unhappy makes you feel as if something has made you unhappy. Still, it is only that you are feeling as you *believe* you will.

For example, the feeling that one is being cheated does not mean that one has actually been cheated. The feeling, in itself, certainly does not mean that one is truly being cheated. In other words, you don't need to be cheated to feel cheated; you only need to believe you are cheated in order to feel unhappy. The feeling that something makes you unhappy doesn't mean that it actually does make you unhappy. You believe it can, so it does. In fact, you don't ever actually need to be *made* unhappy to feel that you are. You only need to *believe* you are being made to be unhappy.

Once a belief is held to be true it is held as "a truth."

The truth that is indeed true, is that unhappiness is merely a belief, and therefore, it can be questioned authentically, innocently and objectively. The objectivity with which we will question that belief is not to be considered as conflicting with or antithetical to the compassion and understanding we have for the suffering person. We *do not*, in fact, and in reality, question the person.

We do not question the person's right to any thought or belief or way of being, or even way of feeling. *What we question is a belief.* By questioning it, we expose it as a mere belief that can, indeed, be questioned.

Unhappiness is a Choice

Although it may not seem obvious at first, people are actually unhappy because they want or choose to be. They believe they should be. They believe it is good and necessary to be unhappy about their experience of not getting what they want, or what they believe they need, or not being who they believe they should be. This attitude is, in effect, the way people choose unhappiness as a feeling. We shall see later how this works, and why this understanding was my basis for developing a method for revealing this dynamic to an unhappy person.

Unhappiness is Not Wrong

An important point to remember about the Option Method Practitioner is that he/she does not believe that people *should be* happy or not unhappy. The Option

Method demonstrates that people choose their emotions, not that they should choose differently. The method helps them recognize that they are not victims of their emotions.

Unhappiness then is defined as the feeling that one's happiness is threatened, that one is helpless to be happy. The belief about the degree of this threat, and how helpless one is, produces exactly the degree of the profundity of the emotions that follow, from slight to extreme.

To be impatient with unhappy persons because they continue in their unhappiness is to deny that they are unhappy because they believe it is a necessary and inescapable truth about themselves. It is to forget that it is not possible for them to be unhappy without that belief. Who would or could ever be unhappy otherwise? All unhappy people believe it is necessary to be unhappy.

The Option Method Questions

* What are you unhappy about?
* What [is it] about that, that makes you unhappy?
* Why are you unhappy about that?
* What are you afraid would happen if you were not unhappy about that? or
* What are you afraid it would mean if you were not unhappy about that?
* Why do you believe it would mean that?

Happiness is not the result of having good things in themselves. What we have always meant by good merely granted us the right to be happy. Happiness is the right to be happy and is the result of not doubting that you have this right—no matter what. All people want to be happy. Happiness is the ultimate desire. Happiness is the prime mover. Happiness is the goal of all desires. The desire for happiness is the sole motivation of all people.

3

The Philosophy Behind the Option Method

Option is from the Latin word for "choice" and the Greek word for "servant." Both roots are quite appropriate for the name of a method whose goal is to serve by helping people realize the role that personal choice plays in their emotional states. This section is an exposition of the basic insights of the Option Method regarding the nature of unhappiness and other emotions.

* All people seek happiness.
* When happiness seems impossible, then all people seek to avoid the greater unhappiness.
* All other things in life are sought as a means to the greatest happiness, or to avoid the greatest unhappiness.

The Primary Operating Principles of Emotions

There is value in knowing how emotions are derived because that knowledge serves to help us in our quest for greater happiness. Since people choose their emotions, they can be happy. *We choose our emotions by means of our beliefs alone.* Once the belief is held, the equivalent emotion necessarily follows. They are the same. The belief is operative as the emotion.

We feel like victims of our emotions because we don't realize that our emotions are determined by our beliefs. We can question those beliefs and then either affirm or change them. We no longer need to feel like victims. We can understand our choices. The truth is that nothing makes you unhappy. Your belief that something does is what causes unhappiness. What you are unhappy about does not make you unhappy; your belief that it can does. Therefore, you can use the Option Method to be happier.

* Emotions are beliefs *about the causes* of happiness and unhappiness.

* "Good for our happiness" or "bad for our happiness" are emotional judgments.

* Whatever emotions you believe you are going to feel in the future, you begin to feel now.

Happiness

* We would always be happy if we did not believe we had to be unhappy.

* Happiness is *believing* you are going to be happy or happier.

* You are happy whenever you believe there is something to be happy about.

* You are happy when you believe something makes you happy.

Fear

* Fear or worry is believing you are going to be unhappy or more unhappy.

* Whenever we believe something is bad for our happiness, we will experience fear. If that thing happens, we get unhappy.

Attitudes

* Attitudes are long held beliefs about the causes of happiness and unhappiness.

* Attitudes are emotional states, which are experienced instantaneously according to perceptions. The perceptions can be subtle or gross.

Believing Happiness is Bad for Us

We are sometimes, it seems, afraid to be happy. We may think we fear happiness, but what we really fear is unhappiness under the name of happiness. We believe that, in some cases, being happy would be self-destructive. We believe that happiness is not true, but a denial of the reality of unhappiness.

We believe it is bad, crazy, unreal, wrong, immoral, sick, inappropriate, unloving, contradictory, etc., not to be unhappy about certain things or losses. These beliefs about happiness are merely ways of believing that if you do not get unhappy when you should, then you will have to be unhappy eventually, anyway. You believe that you must be lying, bad, crazy, or against yourself.

* Because we believe we are bad, we believe that if we feel happy, we might disregard or forsake our truly held values.
* We believe that if we are happy, we will not take care of ourselves or that which or those whom we love.

Believing Unhappiness is Good for Us

We assume that if we are believing that something is bad for a value of ours, it means that we must be unhappy. In order to "be on our side," we get unhappy about our predicament. We have no predicament. Holding values is a freedom. Not all events cooperate with our values. We are actually, merely unhappy about not getting what we want. The truth is we know which things we have decided are against our values. Being happy is being free to know that, without needing to be unhappy to prove it.

Wanting is Happy — Needing is Unhappy

Wanting, or believing in needing, motivates us as humans. We are motivated as we experience our beliefs about happiness and unhappiness. We either want because of our free, self-motivated or self-affirmed choices, or we believe we have needs in order to have happiness or to avoid unhappiness.

* Happy motivation comes from our desires.
* Unhappy motivation comes from believing that we will be unhappy if we don't get what we want or need, or don't avoid what we don't want.

* All desires are freely chosen since no particular desire, or lack of one is necessary to happiness.

WANTING = Happy if you get it or avoid it.

NEEDING = Unhappy if you don't get it or don't avoid it.

What is it that you are always wanting? Your wanting seems to be like nature. First it wants the tide in, then it wants it out. First it wants it raining, then it wants it sunny. But what is unchanging in all of that? Wanting to be happy has never, never changed. Even wanting to be alive comes and goes. Rabbits grow and they die and people and trees are born and they die. Life and death. Even among people. But what beyond that has been unchanging? The wanting to be happy. Obviously the most insistent, persistent imprint of nature on you. Everything in you can change, can come and go. Your wanting this and that. But everything you are and everything you do, you do in order to be happy and that has never stopped. Unceasing, constantly moving, more and more happy.

4

Unhappiness and its Many Forms

Our personal experience of unhappiness is one of suffering. Unhappiness is feeling bad. It is a distressful state for us. Unhappiness is feeling, to some degree, helpless in the face of the "unhappy" event. We feel threatened, hopeless, confused, powerless, lost, or feel that in some way something is "really wrong."

We feel unlucky or otherwise vulnerable to whatever chance brings our way. We worry that we'll never know when misfortune will strike. We're scared, nervous to a degree, and probably "coping" every day, ignoring the fear in the back of our minds. None of us has all the power we need to make sure we will always overcome the things we fear. We suffer in our hearts and minds and bodies from the uncertainty of eventual unhappiness. In a world of suffering people, we choose to believe that some unhappiness is inescapable.

The Value of Feeling Bad

The fundamental dynamic of all unhappiness is the

individual's belief that unhappiness is preferable to happiness. Happiness is seen as some form of craziness or irrationality; it is the belief that being happy is contradictory to a personally held value.

The belief is this:

* "If I wasn't unhappy about it (the loss or possible loss), it would mean that I wanted it to happen."
* "If I wasn't sad (or angry, etc.), it would mean I didn't care."

Anticipating Unhappiness

We feel now what we believe we are going to feel in the future. We feel whatever feelings we believe will happen to us. We feel now whatever we believe it will be natural to feel in the future as a result of something that is happening now. The current event correlates to current emotions only insofar as it relates to imagined future feelings. It is the assumption of the naturalness and inevitability of these that is the real cause of the feelings.

I created two questions to demonstrate this phenomenon:

* "If you believed now that at this time tomorrow you were going to be unhappy, what would you feel now?"
* "If you were to believe now that at this time tomorrow you were going to become very happy, what would you feel now?"

Using Unhappiness as Proof

While most people would probably assert that they want to be happy; in practice they are actually unwilling to be happy under numerous circumstances, and that is precisely why they are unhappy. That people believe it is good to be unhappy is the greatest self-deception they can inflict on themselves.

If "good" can ever have any personal, relevant meaning to a person, it could only be as an emotionally equivalent word for "happiness-causing." Happiness is the goal of all human behavior. Believing something is "good" in a general or moral sense is to believe it must foster happiness in some way. It usually means good for what we want or value. We believe unhappiness is good because it "proves" to us that our desires are consistent with our values and our values are consistent with reality or truth.

No one questions why we believe this. Nor does anyone question why being happy can ever mean that people's values are not exactly what they choose them to be. Remaining happy does not, of course, contradict what we affirm. Being happy does not mean we wanted or approved of our not getting what we wanted, any more than our being healthy does. It makes as much sense to be unhappy when we don't get what we want as it would to make ourselves sick or to hurt ourselves in any way. That we believe that it does make "sense" is our doom.

We are doomed to be unhappy in order to prove that our loss means loss.

Becoming unhappy is like slapping our hand because the fruit we picked was unripe and sour. The truth is, and can only be, that we want what we want as long as we want it, and nothing means otherwise. Not our actions, or gestures, our behavior, nor our other desires or lack thereof. We delude ourselves and begin to feel bad when we accept another's belief or opinion that happiness proves that we don't care about anything.

The Difference Between Sadness and Anger

The two major forms of unhappiness are sadness and anger. Anxiety or worry is fear, another kind of feeling bad which really is the anticipation of feeling bad. This is the fear of feeling bad or unhappy. It is expecting a way that we will sooner or later feel is wrong. It can be expecting to behave in a way that we believe will prove we are against ourselves. We fear bad luck like a paranoiac. We could be expecting an undesirable event, which is a combination of both of the above. We may anticipate a mysteriously caused random accident or bad luck, which we then interpret as meaning that we shouldn't have been happy. We judge this experience to be the "proof" that we were wrong to have been as we were. It is as if the undesirable incident, even only as we anticipate it, "proves" we are bad for ourselves.

We are either sad or angry with this proof. Sadness is

the acceptance of such proof. Sadness is believing that we have proof that we are against ourselves. Anger is feeling wrong for not expecting to be wrong. We feel as if we have been fooled. We seem to be angry with ourselves or with someone else. We are really angry that we allowed ourselves to be mistaken.

The Many Forms of Unhappiness

The various names and forms of unhappiness are related to what is believed to be the cause of those emotions—not the real cause. They range from mild annoyance to livid rage, from slight disappointment to bleak depression. From a nagging feeling of something undone or forgotten to dread of doom, vague worries, demons and suicidal fears. From feeling guilty for another's bad feelings to feeling hated by God. From phobias, things or behaviors we must avoid, to manias, the things or behaviors we must do. Sometimes it is presents itself as feeling stupid or worthless.

These are just a few examples of almost countless forms of unhappiness that we believe are caused by something or someone, phenomena or events, outside ourselves. This section contains a useful glossary of terms and expressions that helps to clarify our *unhappy* experiences from the point of view of the Option Method. These can also serve as a quick reference for summaries and answers to essential questions about the Option Method.

Boredom

A common symptom in response to the belief that there is something we must do to be happy or happier now, and the uncertainty of what it is, or that we will do it when and if we discover it.

Hate is Fear

We respond with hate or fear to that which we believe can cause our unhappiness. To hate unhappiness is also to deny that we simply don't want it, because we believe that unhappiness is something, in itself, to fear. To fear unhappiness is yet another fear. It will never eliminate unhappiness. To find good in unhappiness is also another fearful state wherein we condemn ourselves to believing we actually desire it, and therefore we will have to fear its reappearance because it might be good for us.

Terror

Our belief that something will happen, and when it does, it will cause our unhappiness.

Obligation

The myth that we owe anything to anybody or even to ourselves. If we want to give, we may give. No one should do anything. We do as we choose.

Blame

Identifying the cause of our unhappiness as coming from someone or something outside ourselves.

Guilt

Guilt is feeling bad for not feeling bad when we should. Also it is believing that we will feel bad for not having felt bad. Additionally it is feeling bad because we believe we made someone else feel bad. It is feeling bad for making or allowing ourselves to feel good when we shouldn't. It comes of believing that being happy makes us a bad person.

Enemies

We define enemies as those people who we believe caused or will cause our unhappiness. Neither anyone nor anything ever caused your unhappiness. Our belief that they had that power was the cause. We feared what they did or what happened.

The Option Method Questions

* What are you unhappy about?
* What [is it] about that, that makes you unhappy?
* Why are you unhappy about that?
* What are you afraid would happen if you were not unhappy about that? *or*
* What are you afraid it would mean if you were not unhappy about that?
* Why do you believe it would mean that?

If you blame no one for your sadness, you will remember not to accept blame for their sadness. If you accuse no one of breaking your laws, you will acquit yourself at their indignance. If you are not disappointed that another seems to be lacking virtue, you can never feel insulted when you are judged inadequate by others. If you are not amazed at the ignorance of men, you will always be at peace. If you are not shocked at the destructive practices of mankind and the violence of nature, you will enjoy your own vision.

5

Our Fears

All fear is the fear of unhappiness. Do we fear poverty in itself, or the unhappiness that poverty is believed to bring? In other words: Do we fear being poor, or the unhappiness that we believe accompanies poverty? Do we fear being sick, or the unhappiness that we believe accompanies illness? Is it that we fear loss or the unhappiness that we believe follows loss? Being alone or the unhappiness of being alone which is loneliness?

The Emotion of Fear Versus Caution

By fear we mean the emotional experience, as opposed to a decision and desire to be cautious in order to avoid something. This fear is itself the anticipation of unhappiness. Being afraid is being unhappy at the prospect of an undesirable event. Being afraid is assuming that we will have to be unhappy when this undesirable event takes place.

Event–Belief–Response

All fear and unhappiness is really the fear that unhappiness will happen to us. For example, no person is afraid of being alone, but of being alone and unhappy. No person is afraid of being poor, in itself, but of being an unhappy poor person. No person is afraid of illness, but of being ill and unhappy also. Nobody is afraid of a bear, but of the unhappiness that is assumed (believed) will occur from being hurt by a bear. It is not the pain of the injury that is most frightening but the unhappiness that will follow the injury.

Countless examples follow this essential model. People are afraid that unhappiness will happen to them under certain circumstances. Although many things are worth avoiding, i.e., they are undesirable; the urge to avoid them is not the same as the feeling of fear of their presumed effect on us. The desire to feel well and healthy for all its benefits, is not the same as the belief that if one is ill and vulnerable, unhappiness will necessarily follow.

Fear is the feeling of anxiety that we experience when we are conflicted about what we should or should not do. We experience the feeling of anxiety when we believe that we should be some way that we do not really value. The fear of heights, acrophobia, is an example of unhappy, fearful, conflicted feelings.

The Fear of Heights

The so-called fear of heights is, of course, a misnomer. It is the fear of falling to harm or death. There is for most people a desire for caution at great heights. This desire for caution is not yet a fear or phobia. They are quite aware that they have very limited experience in maintaining stability at great heights or keeping an appropriate distance from an edge or precipice.

While it may be true that the skills needed are little more than what is required to walk or hold one's stance on the ground, many people do not find it attractive to go beyond certain limits. They are not willing to bet their lives on the fact that they may have the skills needed to be safe. Yet when they believe they are wrong to feel this way, and believe that they should not have such strong feelings of caution, they experience what is called the fear of heights. It would seem almost that one should recklessly endanger oneself even though one has no such desire to do so. A person comfortable with his/her own sense of caution, who does not feel challenged to "overcome" his/her so-called fear, will not feel the fear of heights.

The Fear of Unhappiness

The only thing feared is unhappiness. That is all that we fear. Fear means anticipating our unhappiness. Fear, as we are using the word, is an emotion. Fear comes from the belief that if we do not avoid a certain thing, we will become unhappy.

Unhappiness is believing that something can make us a way we are not allowed or supposed to be. Unhappiness is believing that something can make us think, act, or have emotions and desires that we won't want.

Unhappiness, as we have already seen, means to feel bad. To feel unalloyed happiness or undeserving of happiness is the same as feeling that we are bad. The reason, so to speak, that feeling bad feels bad is because of what we believe about "bad."

Bad, whether it is about us, or about what happens to us, means that we *should* feel bad. "Bad" means deserving of punishment. Punishment is anything that can make us, or is supposed to make us, feel unhappy.

For punishment to work as punishment, it must convince us that we don't deserve to feel good or be happy. It must convince us that we deserve to be in pain or to feel unhappy. We must feel bad. If not, then it is not punishment.

We become unhappy when we don't get what we want. When we don't get what we want we feel, in a sense, that we are being punished, as we should be, even if we don't know why.

Unhappiness is believing that something proves we are a way we should not be, and we deserve to feel bad.

Unhappiness is believing that we are bad for ourselves. "Bad for ourselves" means we cannot feel the way we would like to feel. It also means that we cannot be the way we are supposed to be.

Love your wanting. Praise your desires. Be proud of your feelings, and glad for your actions. What moves your hand? Happiness. What sparks your thoughts? Happiness in you. What pulses in your heart with desire? Happiness. What gives those desires names? Happiness.

The Fear of Self

The Option Method makes apparent that what people need in order to be happy is the confidence that their happiness cannot be threatened. They need to know that their happiness can't be taken away. They need to know that they need nothing.

That said, there can be yet another question about the nature of unhappiness: Can we be unhappy without, in some way, believing we can feel in a way other than we want to feel? In other words, can we be afraid or unhappy about anything other than our own *feelings*? The answer is, absolutely not.

Fear and unhappiness follow from the belief that we are going to feel a way we won't like feeling in the future. Feel, in this context, means the emotional experience of feeling bad. We are afraid that the real truth about our future selves is that we will be unhappy and, therefore, against ourselves.

Anxiety, Worry and Guilt

Anxiety or worry is the kind of fear that we have when we believe there is something we need to do; otherwise we can't be happy.

The belief that there is something left undone, needs to be attended to or needs to be fixed is worry. This is the belief that we will be bad for ourselves if we don't worry. The "surety" that we will feel bad if we don't do this thing is the cause of the worry. The doubt that we may not do it intensifies the feeling of anxiety.

The belief that we don't even know what it is, but have to do it anyway, often describes this free-floating anxiety. It is the fear that even if we were to attend to something, that would not be enough. Something has been left undone or something else will still need to be done.

This fear is usually accompanied by the feeling of impending doom or bad luck. It is actually the same fear. The fear that something bad will always be just around the corner is a kind of depression which is being manifested by this anxious belief that we won't or can't do what we have to do to be happy.

Our guilt for not having done what we should have done is the prompter of this fear. If we have already been teaching ourselves that we should feel bad for past negligence and incompetence, we are now ready to promise ourselves that punishment for any future neglect is our expected lot. We are prepared to regret something. The anticipation of that regret is called worry or anxiety.

The important question is, of course, Why do we believe that there is something we must do to be happy? Why do we believe that we will have to be unhappy if we fail to do some good thing?

Fear of Desires

All fear is the fear of unhappiness. We believe a desire to be wrongful because the object of desire will cause unhappiness. We believe that if we got what we wanted, it would be bad because it will cause someone or us unhappiness.

We fear that what is behind some desires is bad for us. We fear that the cause of a desire is not what it should be, even though we don't know what it should be. This is the fear of self-defeating desires. It is also the fear of being crazy.

The Fear of Selfishness

Fearing our motivation is fundamentally the fear of selfishness. We can only have this fear because we believe that it is wrong to be selfish. The only sense in which being selfish could be wrong is that it will somehow ultimately make us unhappy. The fear of mysterious punishment (guilt) follows from this. Secret terror is the fruit of this fear.

We believe selfishness to be wrong because it may lead to behaviors that are harmful and will cause unhappiness to others or to ourselves, or our mysteriously so-called greater good. This greater good is understood to be our greater happiness. This is simply the belief or fear that if we are selfish, we are somehow against our greater happiness.

Fear of Something Wrong with Us

We believe: there is something wrong; deep down inside we have something wrong with us. Each of us fears,

"I'm crazy." The fact that we fear innate craziness, shows how evidently untrue it has to be. Why would we fear a self-destructive urge toward unhappiness if that urge were actually in us? Simply, the fear is full of internal contradictions. We can only fear being self-defeating out of a desire to avoid being self-defeating. Just as we feared unhappiness because of our desire to avoid unhappiness, we likewise fear self-defeat out of our desire to avoid self-defeat.

Fear of Making Mistakes

This is the fear of selfish, self-defeating desires that is reflected in all fear. It feels as though we can't trust ourselves. This fundamental fear is evident in what are called hysteria, paranoia, schizophrenia, or simple anxiety.

Fear Called Hysteria

Hysteria follows from the belief that we have no self-actualizing desires. People seem demanding, selfish. We fear we might not do what we can to be loved by others. We are unhappy about our powerlessness. It feels as if we can never say enough, do enough, or give people enough love to satisfy them. We believe we are lacking passion. We feel as if people don't understand how innocent and loving we really are. We actually feel that the effort that we put forth is almost beyond our true abilities. We struggle to keep up; we experience worry and the fear of regret.

We become quietly angry and resent criticism, especially the nagging urging of others. We don't question ourselves, and we justify ourselves when we are embarrassed by criticism. We find ourselves blaming others for their insensitivity and fussiness.

Fear Called Paranoia

Paranoia follows from the belief that we have self-defeating desires. We fear that we might do something we shouldn't do in order to be loved by others. We feel as if we should not love or want people as much as we do. It seems as though we do, say, or want more than we should. We believe we have too much passion. People *seem* to avoid us, disdain us or hate us. We experience anxiety and the fear of regret.

We believe people can't or won't love the real us. It feels as if people dislike us because they suspect our selfish motives. Ironically, we start to feel as though we have more powers than we use or show. We struggle to play it cool, though we miss the lack of encouragement from others. We secretly question ourselves. Though overtly we justify ourselves when embarrassed by the criticism of others whom we blame for over-sensitivity and ill will.

Fear Called Borderline Personality

The so-called borderline personality comes from the belief in self-neglect, and can cause accident-proneness. If we believe that we won't do what will make us happy,

we will feel like a loser or a martyr. Hysteria and paranoia complement each other in many ways. We can be
"diagnosed" as a hysterical paranoid or a paranoiac hys-
teric. We are judgmentally fussy and monumentally ne-
glectful. We strain out gnats and swallow camels. Image
is extremely important and we confess our tremendous
faults. We fear being hysterical because we are convinced
we are. We have many physical/psychosomatic symptoms
and mental/emotional symptoms as well. We find fault
with most people and yet are envious of their normal suc-
cesses, happiness and luck.

We fear being paranoiac because we believe we are. We
confess to others our delusions of grandeur and egomania,
and we hate ourselves. We think we're unworthy of love,
and yet more worthy of admiration than we are credited
for. We are at once too small and too big. We believe we
are impotent, lazy and a fake. We believe we are brilliant,
driven and cheated. Like most people, we believe we are
a contradiction, only more so.

If it is in your heart, where does it come from?

6

The Good Versus Evil Dilemma

The belief in evil is the belief that people can be against themselves, either against their own will or through their own will. Either possibility is depressing or frightening. The belief in evil is no more than the fear that people can be against their own values, and, therefore, unhappy against their will. The belief that unhappiness in any or all of its forms can happen, and happen to an unwilling person, will cause unhappiness.

No matter how unattractive or dangerous the expressions of unhappy persons may appear, it is still unhappiness not evil. Unhappiness, no matter how expressed, no matter what kind or style or nature, could never in itself cause further unhappiness, save to the fearful. What the fearful *believe* is the true cause of their unhappiness. Although one or many kinds, of unhappiness may touch on our fears or beliefs, unhappiness is still unhappiness, not evil.

The Two Judgments

There are two judgments we can make about unhappiness, either of which is merely another form of unhappiness. These two opinions of unhappiness are the perpetuators of unhappiness. They make unhappiness seem other than what it is, and, therefore, perpetuate the mysteriousness of the phenomenon.

One belief is that unhappiness is good; the other belief is that it is bad. The truth is that unhappiness is simply unhappiness, nothing more, nothing less. Unhappiness is feeling a way we don't like. Unhappiness is not good, nor is it bad.

Our belief that it is good only praises it, and proclaims a value for and attaches usefulness to this very most undesirable state, which we have always wanted to escape. Our belief that it is bad only promotes hate for it and proclaims it to be something fearful and mysterious.

Both attitudes or beliefs fail to acknowledge that unhappiness is merely a belief and an illusion created by our fears. It is not something real or something actually to fear. Our fear that something is real does not make it real. Unhappiness is, at most, undesirable. That we don't want it is the second most honest thing we can say about it. That unhappiness is not real is the most honest and freeing acknowledgment we can make.

The Belief that Bad Things Cause Unhappiness

People describe things as "bad or evil" because those

things are believed to or supposed to cause some kind of unhappiness. They do seem to cause unhappiness precisely because they are believed to be bad.

People cannot get unhappy about something that they do not believe is bad. Likewise, they cannot but be, indeed, must be, unhappy about something they personally believe to be a bad thing or event.

Equivalent and synonymous with the belief that bad things cause unhappiness, is that certain things, events, or behaviors should or should not be happening. This is also the same belief that things can prevent unhappiness or cause it. These kinds of unhappiness range from emotional discomfort to moral outrage, tragic sadness or mental "breakdowns" and trauma. Those things-that-should-not-be are forbidden, and those things-that-should-be are demanded within a particular culture or sub-culture; not only for whatever undesirable or desirable effects they may have, but in order to prevent unhappiness.

Feeling Like a Victim

When we are unhappy we are, in effect, making the claim that bad feelings happen to us. We believe that we would not choose to feel this way, but are instead forced to feel this way by an event rather than the result of our own choice. This is feeling like a victim; and we are deceiving ourselves.

Unhappiness is the experience that what we are feeling or will feel is not what we would freely choose to feel. We do not have to be unhappy. We must acknowledge that whatever we feel or will feel will be what we truly like feeling.

In this frame of reference, we can see that so-called bad feelings come from our believing that our desires are not acceptable.

By using the Option Method, we guiltlessly accept our own desires or lack of them. It turns out that the most common reason we don't accept our initial feelings or desires is that we have learned that we shouldn't. We think those feelings are wrong. Here are some final observations about "the good versus evil dilemma."

Evil

There is no evil. Since by the word "evil" is meant our fear that something can make us unhappy against our will or choice, it does not exist. All unhappiness is caused by the believer's belief that he or she must be unhappy.

Bad

Nothing or no one is bad in itself. Things are bad for something we want or value. Nothing is bad for our happiness; and the unhappiness that comes from our belief in it, lasts only as long as we believe we deserve it.

Fear of Being Evil

Feeling we are evil is believing we are happy when

we shouldn't be, or unhappy when we shouldn't be. The modern version is feeling crazy, self-defeating, sick, etc.

Hatred of Evil People

Believing that another person is evil is the fear (a belief) that he/she causes unhappiness, that the other is wrongly happy or indifferent about another's unhappiness. It is the belief that someone-anyone shouldn't cause unhappiness. The fear of evil people may include the belief that they may desire our unhappiness, and that they can achieve our unhappiness. The belief that there are things or phenomena anywhere in the universe that should not exist is the belief in evil.

Things that Seem Against Us

Because things are destructive to what we love or desire, means neither that they are evil, or not evil. It means that they can be destructive, or that we do not love them, and do not want them.

Since to be truly happy we must believe we can be, we have to see this quality as one of our own, as coming from our real self. We have to know that we wouldn't be wanting to be happy unless it was about to emerge from us. Where we are now and are going to be is up to us now. Where we are now is up for grabs. Our feelings never reflect where we are right now at the moment we are questioning them. They only reflect where we were up until a moment ago.

7

We Cannot be Bad for Ourselves

Unhappiness is the belief in the wrongness of being. To be unhappy is to feel that we are wrong to be who we are. To be angry is to believe we have been wronged. Unhappiness is believing that not everything we do and are is what we believe is best. Unhappiness is believing that we don't always want what is best, the highest good, and the very best for ourselves. Unhappiness is believing that desiring the best is not our only motivation at all times.

When we believe we have to be unhappy, we feel as if we are against ourselves. Our belief in unhappiness is the belief in being wrong for ourselves. In our unhappiness, we believe that what we can want, or think, or feel is in some way bad for ourselves. We are afraid that we are bad or wrong for ourselves, that our way of being could be wrong or bad.

A person thinks: Certain things I do not want to happen may happen or are even now happening. I don't want them to. I feel bad and I am worried and afraid now because I shouldn't be thinking negatively about my life but I should be wanting what is evidently happening—or going to happen anyway. Could I be denying reality? If I am, that is wrong. "I will be unhappy about this" means that in the future when certain things I do not like do happen, I will feel that that is bad for me. But it is wrong to expect misfortune.

It doesn't matter that an undesirable event results from circumstances out of our control or that we think we are its cause or part of its cause. Unhappiness comes when we believe that we now have proof that we are bad for ourselves.

Basically we feel bad when we believe that what we do or think or want or feel means that we are against our own best interests. We are believing that the way we are being is bad, wrong, self-defeating.

This could be the same as believing that we will be a way we shouldn't be, or think a way we shouldn't, or want or feel a way we shouldn't. If we didn't believe that we could be a way that we sometimes "shouldn't," we wouldn't feel unhappy, no matter what else we felt.

All unhappiness is the fear that we harbor a bad attitude toward ourselves. We are afraid that something proves we are bad for ourselves. Finally we have the proof that we are for what we are against, and against what we are for! We are afraid that we have a lousy attitude!

And the fear that we have this bad or self-defeating

attitude is the very distrusting of our own source of our motivation. Namely, we are unhappy when we believe that our very life, our heart, our self is against all that we live for, i.e., our personal happiness.

Happiness is the *freedom* to be as we are, however we are: rich or poor, sick or well, gaining or losing, winning or failing, wanting or not wanting, approving or not approving—forever. Happy is what we are and what we'll be if we don't believe we are wrong to be as we are.

Our Personalities are Self-Created

There is a simple view of a person that is essential to the Option Method attitude. It is that each person creates and shapes his/her own individual personality in all its aspects and apparent complexities using his/her genetically inherited physical attributes. We sustain this view by means of the beliefs we choose to accept as true about ourselves, about other people, about the nature of the world, God—and especially about the belief in evil. The merit of this view becomes obvious in the practice of the Option Method.

We are exactly as we wish to be and choose to be. We are glad to be and don't want to do anything about that. We don't need to, for to do so would be meaningless. We simply won't or can't be other than (gladly) ourselves. Unhappiness is believing, nevertheless, that we should be other than who we are.

Judging Others

It follows, of course, that since we believe we should be different, others should be different also. To believe that another needs to be or should be different is to judge another, and such a judgment is simply an expression of our unhappiness. When we believe others should be different we are manifesting our belief that we also should be different. Just because we do change our minds it doesn't mean we could or should have changed our minds.

For all practical, actual, real-life purposes, we choose what we feel about everything. We only feel bad when we believe that the way we feel is not the way we really feel. It is at these times that we are not glad to feel what we naturally feel. When we believe that we could be at odds with ourselves, could be against what we are for, and for what we are against, we grow depressed, convinced that we are not good for ourselves, and we end up judging ourselves as well.

Choosing Best

All people choose what they believe is best for themselves and can do no other. Given the choice among seemingly good things we will always choose what we believe to be the best choice. Given the choice between what we believe to be good or bad for us, we can only choose the good.

Given the choice among only bad things, we can only choose what we believe is least bad, that which we believe is best. When we do not or cannot decide on a best choice, we, in effect, still choose what we believe is best, i.e., not making a decision. If we choose to make no choice then that is because we believe that no choice is best.

We Are Free

People don't make us unhappy because they are doing what they are doing or not doing it. Our unhappiness is caused by our *belief* that there is a way people should be. There seems, then, to be ways we want people to be. What we believe about people does not, in itself, motivate them or inspire what they believe is best for them. Of course, the same is true for us. We don't have to be what others expect.

Freedom to be Against

We do not have to believe that something is evil, bad or the cause of unhappiness in order to be free to be against it, or not to want it. We are free to be opposed to something simply because we feel it is not completely harmonious with our desire.

Freedom of Taste

We cannot be happy if we believe that we are not allowed our own tastes and preferences in life. We are free not to like whomever or whatever we choose for any reason or no reason. We are also free to change our minds.

Freedom of Choice

We do not ever have to justify or explain our prefer-ences or choices. We may wish privately to explore our motive or rationale. We may choose to explain to gain another's agreement, but we do not have to do so in order to be satisfied that we have the right to our choices.

Choice

To believe that unhappiness is welcome, a good, and natural sign of our caring and sanity, or fear that we will be visited by unhappiness against our will, are the same unhappy belief. We have believed that it is good and natu-rally necessary to be unhappy. We believed that in order to be sane, and, therefore, happier in the long run. We have however, had to fear that we will be unhappy even when we don't want it, because it is natural to our desire not to be crazy.

Life is Perfection
Everything is what it must be.
There is nothing wrong.
Everything is precisely and exactly how it should be.
Everything that exists now has come necessarily from
what caused it.
You have the freedom to change what is perfect.
You may change or wish to change anything that is.
There is nothing wrong in this desire.
Your desires are perfect.

To wake up each day is a direct act of God's gift
of awareness. Only God awakens the sleeper, gives
awareness of happiness, and restores the sick.

God is the only cause of memory for those who forget.
Awareness when given is kept and sustained by
gladness for having it. Gladness allows a person to do
what is necessary to sustain awareness of happiness
and health.

If we are not glad, we forget, we fall asleep.

The Option Method Questions

* What are you unhappy about?
* What [is it] about that, that makes you unhappy?
* Why are you unhappy about that?
* What are you afraid would happen if you were not unhappy about that? *or*
* What are you afraid it would mean if you were not unhappy about that?
* Why do you believe it would mean that?

8

How To Use The Option Method Questions
by Deborah Mendel

When you ask yourself the Option questions, I suggest that you either write them down or say them out loud or do both. This will help you to keep track of your thoughts while you become more familiar with them. In a short time the questions will become "second nature." Eventually you will find yourself *starting* to ask a question and then drop it, because your true or good feelings will already have emerged. "Why do I have to feel bad about this?", will become "why do I have to feel bad . . . ?", will become "why do I have to feel . . . ?", will become "Why do I have . . . ?", will become "why do . . . ?" will become why . . . ?" until finally you say simply "I don't have to feel bad," because you just don't and you'll feel better. All you need is your natural desire for happiness.

The Option Method will help you to begin to break down those "barrier beliefs" that have, over time come between you and your happy heart. Be patient with yourself.

You have spent a lifetime acquiring and cultivating beliefs, which you never realized before are actually contrary to the wisdom within you. Option will help you to uncover the beliefs that don't really serve you, the ones that seem to make you feel a way you would really rather not feel.

So that everyone may use the Option questions in a very personal way, you should replace the word "unhappy" with whatever word best describes the negative feeling you're experiencing that you would like to change. It may be "sad" or "annoyed," "angry" or "worried" or "fearful." Whatever word best describes the bad feeling you feel stuck with, the one you would like to change, use that word.

The purpose of the Option questions is first to help you to *identify* and *clarify* exactly what is bothering you. The questions that follow expose the *belief* behind your emotion or bad feeling. As the questions open the door to your heart, the beliefs you've acquired will fall away and your true feelings will become evident. Knowing who you really are can be easy, can be painless. There is nothing to memorize or study. After all, you are your own best expert.

The first question:

"*What* am I unhappy about?"

Personalize this question. Substitute the word *unhappy* in this question for one that best expresses the bad feeling *you* have that you would like to change. For instance, you may be feeling worried about something. If so, you would ask yourself, "*What* am I worried about?" Clarify your answer. Narrow it down. If, for example, your initial answer to the first question is something like, "I'm worried about my health," that is a very broad answer. You need to narrow it down and be as specific as possible. The closer you get to the core of your feelings, the closer you become to your true heart. This clarifying question will help you to do that.

"What is it *about* that, that makes me unhappy?"

Using the previous example of "worrying about my health," you would now ask yourself, "What is it about my health that I am worried?" Now you are being specific. There are other ways of asking this question, such as, "What about my health worries (bothers, frightens, angers, saddens) me the most?" Your answer may be something like "I know that I don't take care of my health enough. I eat too much of the wrong foods, and I don't get enough exercise. I'm going to become sick if keep this up." To clarify your answer, ask next, "If that were to happen, what would I be most afraid of?" or "If that were to happen, what would be the worst thing about it?" In other words, "If I were to become sick, what would be the worst thing about it?" Remember the answers to such questions are as diverse as we are. The purpose of the questions is to help you get in touch with *your* reasons for being unhappy. This brings us to the next Option question.

The second question:

"*Why* am I unhappy about that?"

You ask yourself this question when you are satisfied that you have clearly identified, to the best of your ability, what it is specifically that is bothering you. It is a simple question, but let's make sure you understand it. "Why" means "for what reason." Therefore, "Why (or for what reason) am I unhappy about that?" is one of the most important questions you may ever ask yourself. This question prompts you to recognize that you have your own very personal reason for feeling the way you feel. Often we get so caught up in our emotions that we have completely forgotten what our original reason was for feeling bad. This wonderful, simple question gives you a renewed opportunity to begin your own self-enlightenment.

To apply this question to our example you would ask, "*Why* am I worried about getting sick?" In other words, "What is *my reason* for worrying about becoming unhealthy?" or "What would I be afraid of or what would it mean to me if I did get sick?" At some point you will find yourself feeling as if you don't know why, that you just always have been *unhappy* (what Bruce Di Marsico called the model word, see Chapter 2, The Option Method Questions, page 31) about it, or that it seems natural to be unhappy. Perhaps you are not aware of any reason. When you ask yourself this second question you may feel somewhat dumbstruck or stuck. This is a natural phenomenon that takes place as we become more aware of our true selves. At this time we are on the threshold of self re-discovery. When this happens, it is time to move on to the third question.

The third question:

>**"What would it mean if I were *not* unhappy about that?"**

Another way of asking this question is, **"What am I afraid would happen if I were *not* unhappy about that?"** This is an extraordinary question, one you may very well never have heard before. Repeat it a few times. You may at first simply feel that this a ridiculous question and that's natural, but let this question into your heart and it will awaken you. Your response finally may be something like, "Well, it wouldn't mean anything, I'd just be happy." If so, you're not really *asking* yourself the question. Ask again. You see, since nothing has been actually forcing you to feel the way you don't like to feel, then up until now you must have had a reason for feeling this way. Until now, you have not exposed or questioned your reasons. You have assumed an unquestioning belief in them without even knowing what they are! You have affirmed it and re-created it as your own. When did you do so? It does not matter. What truly matters now is that through this question you embark on your own spiritual adventure. In other words, "What am I afraid it would mean if I were *not* unhappy about that?" Ask it. Embrace it.

After you have written down or spoken aloud your answer, you will be ready for the fourth Option question.

Take your time. Be satisfied with your answer. If you're feeling a bit confused or uncertain, go back to the first question. It's impossible to get lost on your *own* path. Use the questions as a tool, a flashlight, to light the pathway back to the truth in your own heart. Like the taste in your own mouth, only you can experience it and really know it. Be patient with yourself. You have spent a lifetime establishing and developing beliefs that you have never questioned before in this or any other way. The Option questions, though seemingly simple, are new and foreign to you. Don't rush yourself.

You may find yourself answering the third question with something like, "It would mean I don't care," or "It would mean I am crazy." Continuing the example of worrying about health, you may answer, "If I wasn't worried about being sick I'm afraid that I wouldn't do anything to improve my lifestyle and health now." This answer shows how you are choosing to be worried because if you weren't, it would mean you wouldn't take care of yourself. These kinds of beliefs that employ fear as the source of our motivation are at the core of all unhappiness.

Ask this final question now:

"**Why would it have to mean that?**"

In other words,

"**Why do I believe that being happy would be bad for me right now?**"

Seem too simple? Good! You've got it! The operating principles behind our feelings are fundamentally the same. If you believe something is bad, you feel bad about it. If you believe something is good, you feel good about it. If you believe that something is neither good nor bad, you won't have any feelings one way or the other. Most importantly, if you believe that to feel happy in any given situation would somehow be bad for you, then naturally, you won't feel good.

Remember, you are your own best expert. The invitation that Bruce and I extend to you is to use the Option Method to rediscover *your* personal wisdom and happiness. Apply the Option questions to those emotional problems that you would like to solve right now. Once you lighten your negative emotional load, you will be freer to feel however you want to feel, freer to feel that which is most natural for you to feel, whatever is right for *you*.

You have found and now have all you have ever sought. God. Perfect happiness. Your life. All that is left is for you to do whatever you want. In every moment, as you do your life, think, feel, be, desire . . . You are free. Even if your body becomes tied, your happiness will still be flying within you.

Afterword

The Power of Our Word

by Wendy Dolber

I was very pleased when Deborah Mendel asked me
if I would like to add something to this wonderful book
about the Method. I thought about it long and hard. What
could I add that would help people to use the method to
its fullest? As someone who learned Option at the knee
of Bruce Di Marsico and has been an Option Method
practitioner for over thirty years, I consider myself truly
blessed. The Method is miraculous in its ability to cut
through years of unhappiness and completely change a
person's view of the world. I have had many revelations
over the years in my Option journey. Even now, after all
these years, fresh ways of appreciating the impact of Option happen in my life and my practice. If there were one
thing that I would consider to be essential for success in

using Option to its fullest, I would say it would be to understand the power of our word.

We've all known people who keep their word and people who don't. We tend to gravitate toward those that do and avoid those that don't. There's a kind of trust that we only feel toward those who do as they say. When we apply that principle to ourselves, we tend to think of it in terms of doing what we say. When we say we'll be there at 10 o'clock, we make sure we are there (if we like to keep our word). When we say we'll do something, we make sure we do it. Most of us like ourselves this way and we like the responses we get from others.

Keeping our word goes far beyond doing what we say. When you really think about it, our word defines us. The things we say to ourselves define who we are. It matters what we say to ourselves. The Option Method teaches us to hear our word in a different way. It teaches us that our word, the things we say to ourselves, can make all the difference in the world to our happiness.

So, listen carefully to your word, and know that you are the sole determinant of what your word is. Ask yourself if the voice inside your head is the voice you want to hear. Is it the voice of your best friend, who loves you and wants you to be happy? Or, is it the voice of judgment, fear, need, despair? The Option Method helps us to discriminate between our word and the words of others. Perhaps in our unhappiness, we are echoing voices heard decades ago when we were little children. Perhaps we are echoing the countless voices of fear and sadness that waft through our universe every day. It's natural to hear these voices, but we don't have to honor them. To be happy, we must consistently raise our own voice and hear our word. To be happy, we must know that our word matters.

So listen carefully to the voice inside your head and make sure it is the voice you want to hear. Know that the power of your word is solely within your control and no one else's. Make sure your word nourishes your soul and don't ever allow a lie to go unchallenged. This is your right and your gift. Never underestimate its power!

Notes

Notes

Additional copies of *Unlock Your Happiness With Five Simple Questions: The Option Method* may be ordered through Deborah Mendel at *www.choosehappiness.net*, *www.optionmethod.com* or *Amazon.com*.

ALSO . . .

*Be Happier Now: Your Personal Roadmap
to a Life of Joy and Happiness*
The Option Method Workbook by Deborah Mendel
$19.95

Anyone desiring to learn how to use the Option Method will find this workbook both simple and enlightening. This workbook explains the Option Method questions that were created by her late husband, Bruce Di Marsico. Deborah has created a hands-on tool that is ideal for the novice or experienced Option Method student. The Option Method Workbook may be used alone or in conjunction with Bruce's book and CDs to teach yourself or others how to use the Option Method. She guides you through the process of using each question to help you identify the core beliefs that are keeping you from being happier in life.

The Option Method Workbook will give you the tools and understanding to transform your life. Bruce Di Marsico created his method foremost as a self-help tool. This book instructs you how use the Option Method to help yourself. You are your own best expert. Find your path to happiness using the Option Method.

This workbook may be ordered from Deborah Mendel through *www.choosehappiness.net*, *www.optionmethod.com*, *Amazon.com* or send a check or money order for $19.95 (includes shipping) to: Deborah Mendel, P.O. Box 1192, Walnut Grove, CA 95690. Contact Deborah for quantity discounts.

The Key to a Happy Life
Bruce Di Marsico Presents the Option Method
(35 minute Audio CD)
$12.50

This is the first recording of Bruce Di Marsico to be released. In this live recording originally taped in New York in April 1973, he shares his Method and the philosophy behind it. The timelessness of this lecture is breathtaking.

Discover the real Bruce Di Marsico; not fictional, not mysterious nor elusive, but rather a most kind and gentle man. Bruce explains in his own words how this simple self-help tool can free us from our self–imposed suffering to rediscover our personal wisdom and happiness. He demonstrates through stories and real life examples, how what we believe creates what we feel.

Bruce gently and clearly discusses his Option Method questions. He reveals how asking these questions can help us to uncover and let go of the judgments and beliefs that seem to stand in the way of our happiness. He continues to expand and explain the Method and how unhappiness only seems mysterious.

Learn why we use the Option Method,

". . . We look at ourselves because we don't like the way [our unhappiness] fits. We don't like the way our feelings fit us; they make us uncomfortable."

On "Why ask why?" Bruce says,

". . . We can't assume that everyone feels bad for the same reason . . . and we can't assume that about ourselves. We often do. We assume, 'Hey I'm unhappy for the obvious reasons.' What are the obvious reasons? The obvious reasons are sometimes not so obvious . . ."

Bruce teaches about unhappiness in personal terms,

". . . If I'm not going to see that some belief of mine is causing me to be unhappy, what's the first thing that happens? My finger starts to point . . . before you know it . . . we're blaming everything and everybody for our unhappiness, never looking at a belief that maybe we've outgrown, [a belief] that maybe doesn't fit anymore, [a belief] that maybe we don't need."

This audio CD may be ordered from Deborah Mendel through *www.choosehappiness.net*, *www.optionmethod.com*, *Amazon.com* or send a check or money order for $12.50 (includes shipping) to: Deborah Mendel, P.O. Box 1192, Walnut Grove, CA 95690. Contact Deborah for quantity discounts.

The Happiness Secret: Is Happiness a Choice?
The Option Method Philosophy
(90 minute Audio CD)
$24.95

What role does choice play in our happiness or unhappiness? Do we indeed choose to be unhappy? This was the most common question asked by the Option students who gathered together at Bruce Di Marsico's home for this lecture recorded live in November of 1995, just a few weeks before he passed away. These fortunate students, most of whom had studied at the Option Institute, had no idea that these would be Bruce's last recorded words.

Bruce clarifies what he means by "choice." He explains to his students how our beliefs affect our happiness and unhappiness. Bruce explores the connections between our feelings and our beliefs and just what kind of judgments cause us to feel bad.

Bruce describes how his Option Method works,

"[The Option Method takes unhappiness from] that vague cloud of confusion and that which just happens to you and brings it down to the real dynamics that cause your emotions . . . your beliefs and your judgments."

Bruce explains in this lecture,

". . . Unhappiness happens in the dark, it happens in the half light of reason. The problem is that you think you know that you have to be unhappy. I suggest that it's questionable. What if what you are feeling is just the result of a belief you have?"

Bruce discusses the purpose of the Option Method,

"Why are people afraid to be happy? This is the third question in the Option Method. What are you afraid of if you weren't unhappy about that? This [question] reveals the real reason [one has] for being unhappy."

In this lecture, his last before his death on December 4, 1995, Bruce shares with friends and students his kind understanding of human nature and happiness. Discover the root cause of your unhappiness through Bruce's profound insights.

This audio CD set may be ordered from Deborah Mendel through *www.choosehappiness.net*, *www.option-method.com*, *Amazon.com* or send a check or money order for $24.95 (includes shipping) to: Deborah Mendel, P.O. Box 1192, Walnut Grove, CA 95690. Contact Deborah for quantity discounts.

Books and Tapes by Mandy Evans

Emotional Options: A Handbook For Happiness

$11.95

Order from *Amazon.com* or call toll free 1-800-431-1579.

In **Emotional Options** you will find a simple, step-by-step method to free yourself from beliefs you hold that affect your health and happiness—beliefs that limit your ability to love and be loved, beliefs that keep you from making healthy choices in life. Learn how to ask yourself the questions that will release your knowing. When you discover that what you believe is no longer true for you, you dissolve feelings of anger, fear, and doubt that have seemed inevitable—often for years. The result is happiness!

"It's beautiful. I finished it eager for more, much more!"
—Bruce Di Marsico, founder of The Option Method

Travelling Free:
How to Recover From the Past by Changing Your Beliefs

$14.00

Order from *Amazon.com* or call toll free 1-800-431-1579.

"Travelling Free gives insight into freedom from victimization through outworn memories—to use your memories without allowing your memories to use you."
—Deepak Chopra, MD, author of *The Seven Spiritual Laws of Success*

"A valuable tool for those seeking peace and direction." —Bernie Siegel, MD, author of *Love, Medicine and Miracles*

"*Travelling Free* bridges the gap between the psychological approach to wellness and the recovery model of "twelve-step" programs. The simple, yet creative exercises can be done by anyone, anywhere." —*East West Journal*

"In *Travelling Free* counselor Mandy Evans addresses one of the most challenging issues of the recovery process: how to move from naming your pain to changing your beliefs and your life. Evans tells us that, if we want to change our lives, we need only turn, perhaps ever so slightly, and take the very next step in a new direction. It's never ever too late to change our course and create a new life." —*Body, Mind and Spirit Magazine*

"Mandy Evans' work with belief systems is strong and clear. She helps people overcome their self-defeating beliefs in an empowering way." —John Gray, author of *Men Are From Mars, Women are From Venus*

Books by Frank Mosca, Ph.D.

*Joywords: An Invitation to Happiness
through an Introduction to the Option Method*
$11.95

Order from *Amazon.com* or *www.frank-mosca.com* or *www.frankmosca.net* or call 631-843-4115.

Joywords is an introduction to the Option Method that utilizes both a step by step conceptual framework and actual edited dialogues with nine people who profited from this educational experience. You will find issues of panic attacks, sexual abuse, martial discord, failing health, loss of direction in life, breaking free from the constraints of the opinions of others, and fear of death. There are no limits to how happy you can become with this method, except the one's that you presently hold to be true. This work invites you to come to the fullest realization of your potential to live your life in joy.

The Option Method Joybuilding Workbook
$15.32

Order from *Amazon.com* or *www.frank-mosca.com* or *www.frankmosca.net* or call 631-843-4115.

This book unravels the mysteries of how we get unhappy and shows you how to get past your specific problems and get more joy in your life, right now! Its literally a map through all the pain and suffering, the dead ends, the unwanted compromises, the broken relationships, and all the many disappointments that plague our lives. Step by step you are led through a re-education of your under-standing about not only unhappiness, but also happiness. *Joybuilding* is filled with useful examples, exercises and detailed, down to earth instructions on how to use this breakthrough approach called the Option Method.

The Unbearable Wrongness of Being:
Exploring and Getting Beyond the Myth of Unhappiness
$13.95
Order from *Amazon.com* or *www.frank-mosca.com* or *www.frankmosca.net* or call 631-843-4115.

The Unbearable Wrongness of Being is an exploration of the Option Method perspective through the device of literary vignettes taken from classic literature and altered to create an Option dialogue in each story. Join these fic-tional characters on a journey of discovery and find your-self opening the door to greater joy along with them!

The Godspeak
A story of self-discovery
$14.95
Order from *Amazon.com* or *www.frank-mosca.com* or *www.frankmosca.net* or call 631-843-4115.

A journey of self discovery that includes spies, love, sex conspiracies. Follow Dan Ferino as he unravels a mystery that begins with a physicist's death. Join him in a chase across four continents against time as he seeks to save the world and more deeply to find meaning for himself. His discoveries will be yours as well; his self resolution will be a model for your own personal transformation.

"After my own writings, I turn to Frank Mosca's works as the best description of the Option Method." —Bruce M. Di Marsico

"I have found your work outstanding. You have a real gift for effective metaphors and catchy phrases that I admire . . . I am so enthusiastic about your work . . . I consider your work profound, entrancing, and successfully offering a brilliant answer to one of the most urgent problems of our times: why are human beings so unhappy." —Ken Keyes, author and creator of the *Living Love Method*